SAVING AMERICAN CROCODILES

by Martha London

T0014923

FOCUS READERS.

NAVIGATOR

WWW.FOCUSREADERS.COM

Focus Readers is distributed by North Star Editions:
sales@northstareditions.com | 888-417-0195

Produced for Focus Readers by Red Line Editorial.

Content Consultant: Christopher Murray, PhD, Assistant Professor of Biological Sciences, Southeastern Louisiana University

Photographs ©: iStockphoto, cover, 1, 13, 16–17; Shutterstock Images, 4–5, 7, 10–11, 19, 21, 22–23; Claudio Contreras/NaturePL/Science Source, 9; S. Cortell/National Park Service/Everglades National Park, 15; Red Line Editorial, 25; Roy Wood/National Park Service/Everglades National Park, 27; Jeffrey W. Lang/Science Source, 29

Library of Congress Cataloging-in-Publication Data
Names: London, Martha, author.
Title: Saving American crocodiles / Martha London.
Description: Lake Elmo, MN : Focus Readers, [2021] | Series: Saving animals |
   Includes index. | Audience: Grades 4-6
Identifiers: LCCN 2020005912 (print) | LCCN 2020005913 (ebook) | ISBN
   9781644933848 (hardcover) | ISBN 9781644934609 (paperback) | ISBN
   9781644936122 (pdf) | ISBN 9781644935361 (ebook)
Subjects: LCSH: American crocodile--Conservation--Juvenile literature.
Classification: LCC QL666.C925 L66 2021 (print) | LCC QL666.C925 (ebook) |
   DDC 597.98/2--dc23
LC record available at https://lccn.loc.gov/2020005912
LC ebook record available at https://lccn.loc.gov/2020005913

Printed in the United States of America
Mankato, MN
012021

ABOUT THE AUTHOR

Martha London writes books for young readers. When she isn't writing, you can find her hiking in the woods.

TABLE OF CONTENTS

CHAPTER 1

ALONG THE COAST

American crocodiles are large reptiles. These animals often grow to lengths of more than 13 feet (4.0 m). Like other reptiles, crocodiles are cold-blooded. They depend on outside temperatures to keep warm. For this reason, American crocodiles live in areas that are warm all year.

American crocodiles can weigh as much as 2,000 pounds (900 kg).

American crocodiles live on the coasts of Central America and northern South America. They also can be found in the Caribbean. Some live in southern Florida, too. Many live in fresh water. Others live where fresh water and salt water meet, such as in **mangrove** swamps.

STAYING HIDDEN

American crocodiles can see well at night. They see through their clear eyelids. A crocodile's eyes, ears, and nose are on top of its head. As a result, American crocodiles can see, hear, and breathe while mostly underwater. This ability allows them to hide from other animals. Crocodiles wait for prey to come close. Then they attack.

During the day, American crocodiles often try to take in heat. They may find warm water to swim in. Or they may rest in the sun. At night, crocodiles feed. They are powerful predators. They only eat animals, including fish, crabs, and snakes. Without crocodiles in the **food web**, many **ecosystems** would change.

AMERICAN CROCODILE RANGE

NORTH AMERICA

ATLANTIC OCEAN

CARIBBEAN ISLANDS

PACIFIC OCEAN

CARIBBEAN SEA

CENTRAL AMERICA

N
W E
S

SOUTH AMERICA

SURVIVING THE DRY SEASON

American crocodiles live in tropical climates. These climates feature wet seasons and dry seasons. During part of the year, tropical areas receive large amounts of rain. For the other part of the year, **habitats** dry up. Food becomes harder to find. However, American crocodiles are well suited to this climate.

For example, American crocodiles break down their food slowly. They also store fat in their tails. During dry months, crocodiles use the energy stored in their tails to stay healthy. For these reasons, American crocodiles can survive for months without food.

Dry seasons can also be extremely hot. In response, crocodiles dig holes into the sides

American crocodiles have strong tails that help them swim.

of shores. The mud is cool and damp. It keeps the crocodiles cool as well. These holes also let crocodiles spend time out of the sun.

CHAPTER 2

FOOD WEBS

American crocodiles play important roles in their ecosystems. For example, crocodiles dig holes and create mounds of dirt. They use these holes in different ways. The holes keep crocodiles cool. They are also a place to rest. But these holes help other animals, too. When it rains, the holes fill with water.

Many kinds of crocodiles dig burrows to survive dry seasons.

11

The holes remain wet even during long periods with little rain. Other animals use this water to survive.

In every ecosystem, plants and animals are connected. All of these life-forms play certain roles. For instance, many plants are known as producers. This means they create food for themselves. In contrast, certain animals eat those plants. Certain animals also eat other animals. Animals that eat plants or animals are known as consumers. Producers and consumers form parts of a food web.

American crocodiles are important animals in their food web. For example, crocodile waste provides nutrients for

Like American crocodiles, raccoons often find their food in or near the water.

plants. Nutrients help plants grow. Those plants provide food for other animals in the area.

Young American crocodiles are a food source for certain consumers. Their predators include birds and raccoons. American crocodiles are consumers, too.

In fact, adult American crocodiles are known as apex predators. This means that the adult crocodiles face few threats from other animals. American crocodiles eat a wide variety of prey. Their diet includes raccoons, opossums, and fish. As predators, the crocodiles limit the numbers of these animals.

The animals that crocodiles eat are also consumers. For example, opossums eat insects, eggs, and plants. Fish eat aquatic plants and other fish. Raccoons eat eggs and small animals such as frogs. An increase in raccoons could cause a decrease in frogs. And a decrease in frogs could affect the food web in other ways.

An American crocodile preys on an eel.

By limiting the numbers of other animals, American crocodiles help maintain the balance of the whole ecosystem.

CHAPTER 3

LIMITED RANGE

Between the 1930s and 1960s, the number of American crocodiles dropped. People hunted large numbers of them. The animal's skin was valuable. People made clothing out of it. In the 1970s, American crocodile numbers grew in some areas. But hunting remains a threat for many crocodiles.

Crocodile hide is used to make a variety of products, including bags, boots, belts, and hats.

Habitat loss is another major threat. For instance, many people want to live near the ocean. So, they build new homes in coastal areas. The coasts are also popular with tourists. To serve tourists, companies build hotels on these beaches. In addition, some companies use mangrove swamps to farm shrimp. Other companies fish heavily in certain waters. All of these activities can destroy the habitats of American crocodiles. When crocodiles lose their homes, they struggle to survive.

Human actions are also changing the waters in American crocodiles' habitats. For example, farmers often use chemicals

Human development over American crocodile habitat has been the main reason for the drop in crocodiles in Florida.

on their crops. The chemicals can help crops grow. But rainwater washes the chemicals away. The water flows into streams and rivers. Then it flows into other bodies of water, such as wetlands.

Rainwater that reaches streams and wetlands is called runoff. The chemicals from runoff pollute the water. American crocodiles live in many of these areas. But they may not survive in polluted water.

Climate change is affecting crocodiles' waters as well. This crisis is raising

SHY REPTILES

American crocodiles are shy. They tend to avoid humans as much as possible. In areas such as Florida, crocodile numbers are increasing. People are also living closer to where the crocodiles live. In these areas, people and crocodiles may meet more often. Scientists say people and crocodiles can live together. But they say people need to leave crocodiles alone.

People use billions of pounds of farm chemicals every year. These chemicals are known as pesticides.

average water temperatures around the world. Crocodile eggs can only survive in certain temperatures. Climate change may make waters too warm for these eggs. As a result, American crocodiles may struggle to reproduce.

CHAPTER 4

REASON TO HOPE

Many **conservation** groups are working to help American crocodiles. Some of their efforts have succeeded. In the 1970s, for example, approximately 300 crocodiles were living in Florida. In response, the US government listed American crocodiles as **endangered** in 1975.

American crocodile numbers in Costa Rica and the Dominican Republic are especially healthy.

To help, the US government supported studies of American crocodiles. These studies found areas where the crocodiles nested. The government protected land that was home to three nesting areas. Protecting this land helped new crocodiles hatch and grow safely.

UNLIKELY HELPERS

Turkey Point Nuclear Power Plant is in Florida. Workers built **canals** to cool the power plant. Fresh water runs through these canals. For this reason, American crocodiles began nesting in the canals. In the 1980s, leaders at the power plant decided to help. They formed a crocodile team. The team tags baby crocodiles. When the babies grow up, the team brings them to reserves.

At the same time, some crocodile habitats had already been destroyed. People had been draining water from the Florida Everglades for decades. The water helped develop several cities in Florida.

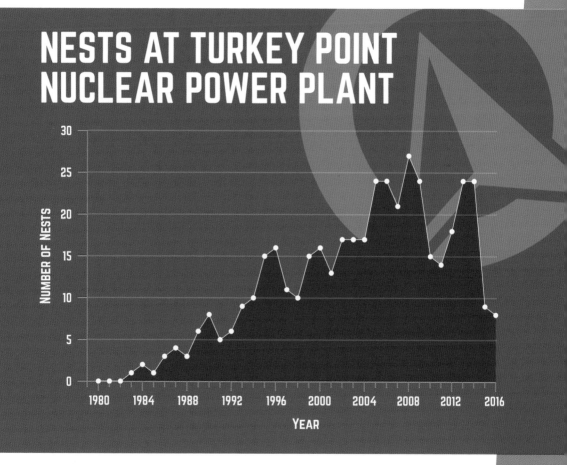

NESTS AT TURKEY POINT NUCLEAR POWER PLANT

However, the wetlands had been home to many American crocodiles. With less water, the Everglades could not support as many crocodiles.

Two American Indian nations, the US government, and Florida's state government took action. They made a plan to restore the Everglades. In 2000, workers started bringing more fresh water into the area. Scientists believed this would keep young crocodiles healthy.

Protecting and restoring crocodile homes worked. By 2007, there were approximately 2,000 crocodiles in Florida. This number was close to the original size of the population. That

An American crocodile basks in the sun in the Florida Everglades.

year, the US government took American crocodiles off the endangered list.

Scientists continue to study American crocodiles. Many track the animals. Some shine flashlights at night. Crocodile eyes reflect the light. Then scientists count how many eyes they see. This number suggests how many crocodiles live in a certain area. Scientists can learn which crocodile groups are healthy.

Scientists also use radio signals to track crocodiles. First, scientists place a small device on the crocodile. This device sends out signals. Scientists' computers receive these signals. That information tells them where the crocodile travels and spends its time. Those areas are most important to protect.

In addition, some countries have crocodile farms. These countries include Cuba and the Dominican Republic. Scientists raise American crocodiles in controlled areas. They keep the animals safe as they grow. When the crocodiles are big enough, scientists release them. Scientists take the crocodiles to existing

A scientist attaches radio trackers to baby American crocodiles.

habitats. In this way, crocodiles return to their original habitats.

American crocodiles will continue to face a number of dangers. Even so, much of the hard work has paid off. And people will keep working to protect American crocodiles.

FOCUS ON
SAVING AMERICAN CROCODILES

Write your answers on a separate piece of paper.

1. Write a paragraph that explains the key ideas from Chapter 3.

2. What do you think are the most important actions people can take to help American crocodiles? Why?

3. What human-made areas have American crocodiles been found nesting in?

    A. mangrove swamps

    B. hotels

    C. canals

4. Why do scientists say that people and American crocodiles can live together?

    A. American crocodiles are shy and likely to stay away from people.

    B. American crocodiles are too weak to hurt people.

    C. American crocodiles are so rare that people will never see them.

Answer key on page 32.

GLOSSARY

canals
Human-made waterways.

climate change
A human-caused global crisis involving long-term changes in Earth's temperature and weather patterns.

conservation
The careful protection of plants, animals, and natural resources so they are not lost or wasted.

ecosystems
Communities of living things and how they interact with their surrounding environments.

endangered
In danger of dying out.

food web
The feeding relationships among different living things.

habitats
The types of places where plants or animals normally grow or live.

mangrove
A type of tree or plant that grows in coastal areas where fresh water and salt water mix.

TO LEARN MORE

BOOKS

Mooney, Carla. *American Alligator*. Minneapolis: Abdo Publishing, 2017.

Rake, Matthew. *Scaly, Slippery Creatures*. Minneapolis: Lerner Publishing Group, 2016.

Spalding, Maddie. *Everglades National Park*. Minneapolis: Abdo Publishing, 2017.

NOTE TO EDUCATORS

Visit **www.focusreaders.com** to find lesson plans, activities, links, and other resources related to this title.

INDEX